My TRUTH

THE PAIN BEHIND THE MAKEUP

Dr. SHIRLEY PEOPLES

Published and distributed in the United States by Dr. Shirley Peoples, Long Island, New York

Unless otherwise stated, scripture is quoted from the New King James Bible found on www.biblegateway.com

Book Coach – Robin E. Devonish
Cover Design – Okomota
Editing and Layout – Pen Publish Profit, LLC
Interior Design – Istvan Szabo, Ifj.
ISBN 13: 979-8-9864018-1-2
LCCN: 2022911033

Printed in the United States of America

ACKNOWLEDGMENTS

It is with the sincere gratitude and words that I am unable to articulate for my profound love and appreciation to my Lord and Savior Jesus Christ. Lord, thank you for who you are to me.

It is with a sense of overwhelming joy to my amazing sons that I recognize Stephen, Marquis Joel, and Charlie who are my abundant gifts from God. Throughout the years, your encouraging reassurance of, "of course Mom, you can do this", gave me comfort and strength of embracing the valuable things in life. As a mother, I am so incredibly proud of the men you have become.

I appreciate you Kendra (Kizzy) for your unselfish, unconditional love. I am overwhelmed with thankfulness for my sisters Doreen, Donna, Shirell, Adrianne, and a host of other family and friends for their support and love. I am reminded of Teshania Blackwell, Pastor and Lady Trent, Catherine Hunt, Davida, and Misha who stood with me through years of opposition, adversity, and affliction. These special vessels represent what it means to be in covenant. You loved me beyond my human faults.

Thank you Paul M. Robinson for pushing me to my next through the Activation Academy.

I give honor to my spiritual fathers, the late great Apostle John H. Boyd, Sr., and Pastor Leo Stallworth who challenged me to go higher, laying the groundwork, and birthing in my apostolic teaching. Your leadership and legacy still live on and have never been forgotten. Thank you so much.

Giving honor to my spiritual mothers, Dr. Gail E. Johnson, Donna Lovell for always being a beacon of light and committed to being there for me. #Mom 4 life!

I also would like to thank Dr. Lord Michael Hunt an iconic intercessor, and Pastor Campbell. Thank you Dr. Tonya Williams for your endless love and support. Finally to the five-fold ministry gifts, thank you for stirring up the gift that I never knew was in me. The deposits you have made in my life birthed confidence in me and allowed me to believe what I could not see or discern. You have been an asset in my life. Again, praising God for the vessels He saw fit to align my path for me to be where I am today.

DEDICATION

My Truth is dedicated to my mother, Shirley I. Foster aka Sugar Mama. I am grateful to my heavenly Father for not only blessing her to be my mother but having her as a mentor. She was a woman of great influence. Her strength, courage, integrity, and being a model in my life allowed me to grow into the stature of woman that I am. Her lifestyle was one of true forgiveness – the kind the Bible references. It is now through the grace of the Most High God that I too, can walk out my journey in forgiveness and healing. Mom, I LOVE YOU!

PRELUDE

"...A thief is only there to steal and kill and destroy. I came so they can have real and eternal life, more and better life than they ever dreamed of."

–John 10:10 MSG

It's all happy, sad and weird that this scripture applies to the believer long before learning, confessing and believing that Jesus is Lord. Interestingly, God knew us before we were born. He knew who would confess and who He would be in relationship with. He knew who would be the apostles, prophets, evangelists, pastors and teachers. What's also interesting is that Satan knew the same thing and would use people, places, and things to thwart the plans of God. If unaware, one can run become the mouse that constantly runs in the spinning wheel thinking it will get to a destination.

I was born to the parents of Jimmy and Shirley Foster. Our family (parents and three sisters) resided in Brooklyn New York. We were a black middle-class family where my father had two jobs with the New York City Housing Authority and at Mount Sinai Hospital in Manhattan as a Nurse. My mother worked at the Post Office. My parents were also homeowners in the Bedford-Stuyvesant section of Brooklyn who also had an entrepreneurial bug.

If you have ever heard the word, 'Juke Joint,' that is what we had in the basement of our home. Every Saturday, people would come to eat, drink, dance and have a good time with each other. My dad forbade my sisters and me to come downstairs or be involved in any way. However, like many children I was curious and would sneak to see what was going on. My dad had a heart for the youth and would also try to reach them to do the right thing by talking to and feeding them a meal so they would get off the street for a few hours. In our neighborhood, my father was considered a good one.

As a family we went on outings and my father encouraged us to have a love for the Arts. One day dad learned about a talent show/competition happening at the school nearby. My sisters and I were encouraged to audition and perform.

There was a lot going on in 1976, it was an exciting year for me. It was a bi-centennial year and I was turning 10 years old. Gang activity was popular, drugs were rampant but my parents did their best to keep us shielded. There were also cops and politicians who formed alliances to do what was bad for the community.

On the night of the talent show at P.S. 289, my sisters and I were excited because we won 1st place in the competition. As a family, we were attempting to walk home happily to celebrate the win. My dad was a man of conviction and did his best to do what was right by others. However, there were people, places and things that wanted him to do otherwise.

Dishonest Damien was our area politician who appeared clean and pristine on the outside but was dark and deadly on the inside. He was a businessman and community leader who many looked up to and the classic example of the term of wolf in sheep's clothing.

As before stated, my father's place was a safe haven for gang members to come and be in a positive environment. Sadly, Dishonest Damien had other plans and approached my father about using his 'Juke Joint' as a hub to selling drugs and having the gang members to sell them. My father firmly refused.

As we began to walk home, a group of people started yelling at us, calling us names, throwing objects, etc. I couldn't understand why. However, my dad sprung into protection mode and told my mom to take me and my sister's home. My sisters listened and ran home. My mom and I decided that we weren't going to leave my father.

He began arguing with one of the people yelling at him, a fight ensued, and I stood there as I watched the mob of people beat my father within an inch of his life. Jimmy Foster was 35 years old when he passed in the hospital from being in a coma.

The situations and circumstances that we are exposed to or experience as a child affect our decisions when we become an adult. Think about it for a moment, if a child grows up with a parent who was addicted to drugs, either they will follow the same path or they will make a vow to never use drugs in their life.

I can go on further to say that traumatic experiences, such as the sudden loss of a parent, can have us searching for who they were in our relationships and connections with people.

I was a daddy's girl and knew that I wanted to grow up and marry a man just like him.

Again, God knows who will confess Him and desire a relationship. However, my life choices would prove to be challenging to get to the point of where I am today, which is 'Sold Out' to Jesus.

INTRODUCTION

The Bible says, "The truth shall make you free." I believe that this statement is true, not only facing inward truth, but outward. What do I mean by this statement? We all must get to a place where we are telling our stories so others can gain their freedom.

When we go through life issues, experience pain, make mistakes or do things we are ashamed of, we tend to shy away, hide or put on a mask from what happened. The consequences of hiding can result in:

- ✓ Addictive behaviors
- ✓ Anger
- ✓ Depression
- ✓ Feelings of abandonment
- ✓ Feelings of rejection
- ✓ Hopelessness
- ✓ Mental turmoil
- ✓ The list goes on...

To live in a broken place is not God's will, purpose or destiny for our lives. His ultimate goal is to guide us in removing the masks in our life, and heal and restore us back to Him.

<u>What is a Mask?</u>

A mask is a face covering to protect, shield or disguise one's face from harm. They are used in theatre productions, medical procedures, sports, and other occupations. Masks are also used as a form of armor and to keep one's true face from being revealed.

Masks definitely serves many purposes for good. However, they also mask hurt, secrets, and most of what is contrary to God and His word concerning us.

I've decided to be transparent about 'My Truth!' Why?

- ✓ I want to show how God's grace, love and patience, sustained me during all my trials and tribulations
- ✓ I want to show how obeying God brings both revelation and transformation
- ✓ I want you to know that you're not alone and we all have a story

Thank you for reading my story. Know that life or circumstances that happen may be a 'Sad Story,' at the moment, but it's also an opportunity for Jesus Christ to show His victories through you.

God Bless You...

CONTENTS

CHAPTER ONE

ARTLESS LOVE

> And above all things have fervent love for one another, for "love will cover a multitude of sins." (1 Peter 4:8)

We know the word love relates, to God, your children, your spouse or significant other and your extended family. Sadly, family often commits hurt or sin toward one another that can possibly scar a person for life.

As a little girl, about five years old, I remember often going to my aunt's house with my mother. Through her marriage, my aunt had a nephew named Secretive Stan who I played with. When that young, you just want to have fun with no understanding that some games are masked in wrong activity. However, Stan would always say, "Let's Play House." Sadly, too many of us know the game of playing mommy and daddy with props. It's usually done in a room with the door closed, without supervision and the illusion that the couple is in love. While that scenario works with an adult married couple, with children it's a lure tactic for abuse and molestation.

Our place to play was in the closet and Secretive Stan had me touching his genitals while he stood there and made weird noises. What did I know? I was a little girl playing with her 12 year old cousin and thought everything was part of the fun. He said, "It's was our secret." Does that sound familiar? At some point, I began asking questions with adults in my family about playing house and the closet visits suddenly stopped.

Experiences like those often open a child up to certain behaviors and curiosities that follows them into teenage and adulthood.

<u>Open</u>

Webster's Dictionary defines **artless love** as "free from guile or craft: sincerely simple."

This definition is the best way I can explain me at one time in my life. At nineteen years old to be exact. I applied for a job at a college and was hired to do clerical work in the Bursars Office. I didn't make a lot of money, but I made due.

While on the job, I became friendly with a young lady named Jessica. She was a pretty, well-spoken, intelligent, African American girl who stood 5'7, had long flowing hair with a slender build. By the texture of her hair, she looked like she was mixed with another nationality. We made it our ritual to do lunch together and became quite friendly outside of the job.

Jessica, Jeff, and Jay

Looking at her made the lifestyle of glamour, glitz, and money, and the perks connected, attractive. I observed how she came to work dressed in designer clothes and handbags. I knew that we didn't make enough money, but I would soon find out how she could afford it all.

One night Jessica invited me to a club in Manhattan. As I entered the door, I gave her name and was escorted to a VIP section where she was having a good time with other friends. I was officially introduced to living the good life. Top shelf liquor like Moet and Pipers was flowing, the music was pumping, and we had a good time. That night I found out that Jessica had a boyfriend who was a drug kingpin named Jay, and he introduced me to his friend Jeff. I decided I wanted and enjoyed those same perks but had no clue about the danger behind the scenes.

The truth was Jessica didn't need to work or date a drug dealer. Her family was very wealthy as they were owners of a multi-million dollar, famous hair care line that many within the African American community used in their homes.

Just like Jessica, I became good at the game. I learned quickly how to live two lives, one with my family and another with my friends. Jeff and I were hot and heavy. Jessica and I remained close hanging out and going on shopping sprees. I was his main girl who was privileged and granted access to everything, even his drugs. I became a frequent recreational drug user with coolies (cocaine inside cigarette tobacco) and snorting cocaine.

One must understand that when dating a drug dealer it's not easy to leave, but being in a relationship with the main drug lord there's no way out except through death. You know and have seen too much which gained their trust. No one really knew me!

As I look back, God was at work in my life by making a way of escape for me one evening. As I said earlier, the only way out is death.

One evening, I dropped Jessica to the airport so she could catch a flight to D.C. to meet Jay. I was supposed to attend the trip but opted not to go. Though we made it to the airport, we were too late because Jessica missed her flight.

Jay and Jeff were to pick Jessica up from the airport but receive word that her flight was missed. The guys went back to the hotel to wait. Upon their arrival, someone was lurking and killed both of them. No one heard a gunshot so the authorities determined they were killed with silencers on the gun. Jessica's life was spared due to missing that flight.

I was devastated as Jeff and I were together for nearly two years. You would think I was done with being in a relationship with someone who led a dangerous lifestyle. Unfortunately, I didn't learn my lesson!

Heart Crusher Corey

I remember the day I met Corey. We were introduced at a club in Brooklyn by my sister Marsha. He was a handsome, dark, beautiful teeth having man with a contagious smile. He stood at 6'2 with a medium muscular build and broad shoulders. He was Panamanian and spoke English, Spanish, and French. By day, he worked for an energy company. At night, weekends, and in between, he was a lucrative drug dealer. I was his main girl.

Our relationship was serious and became more so once I found out I was pregnant. We talked about marriage but the conversations became real once I shared the news.

One day Corey came and told me that he needed to go and visit his family in Panama. He would be gone for two months and that I should begin planning our wedding to take place when he returned. The goal was to reserve a yacht for our nuptials. I was excited to be having our baby and getting married.

Two months, turned into four months. I was due to have our baby and Corey hadn't returned. At this point, I no longer heard from him. Not a phone call or a letter, Corey never returned to the United States. I was hurt, embarrassed, and ashamed and had to tell people there wasn't going to be a wedding. I fell into a depression. I contemplated suicide and possibly aborting the baby. My friend talked me out of walking into the abortion clinic. At this time, thinking about God was the furthest thing in my life and I refused to step foot in a church. However, I needed help so I called my sister and told her what I was feeling and thinking. She replied, "Shirley, come to the gospel tent service with my church."

I said, "You know I'm not stepping foot into any church."

She replied, "No Shirley, its outside under a tent. Just come and you will see."

I agreed, I met her there and that night I gave my life to Jesus Christ. It was the year 1989.

Charismatic Chris

While I was six months pregnant with Corey's child, I met Chris. I was working for a popular car rental company as their manager of reservations. Chris had rented a car but didn't bring it back on the date specified. When that happened, part of my responsibility was to call the driver and see how we can get the car back or determine if the authorities needed to be called.

When I called Chris and left a message, he immediately returned the call. He shared it was an innocent mistake with other flirtatious and sly talk. Before I knew it, I was agreeing to meet him in person. I'm not sure why I agreed, but I did. I also didn't share over the phone that I was pregnant.

We met at a neutral place. I thought he was cute, sound sexy on the phone but wasn't my type. Standing at 5'10, with a nicely built body, I preferred men with darker skin. However, he was nice.

I immediately told Chris that I was having a baby. He didn't believe me because I wasn't showing. While we were talking, a friend of mine walked into the establishment and sparked a conversation. She was six months pregnant and showing. To confirm what I shared, he touched my stomach. With shock and mouth opened wide, he said, "You're pregnant!" Once he got over the moment, he didn't storm out or shun me. Chris was kind and kept the conversation going. I thought that was cool of him.

We remained friends and spoke on the telephone. Chris was there as a great comfort and support when I realized that Corey wasn't coming back and I would have to deliver my baby alone. I did, and my first son was born a whopping 10 pounds.

Chris and I became closer and began dating. He was a kind man who was in my corner. When my son turned one year old, Chris didn't formally propose but expressed his interest in us being a family. His words were, "I would be a good father."

My sister Clara invited Chris to Mega-Mega Ministries for a church service and Chris gave his life to the Lord as well.

We began planning our wedding. However, I had to help my mother with a financial situation. Chris had no problem with agreeing to help my mom, so we went to the justice of the peace. In April of 1991 we came together in holy matrimony.

Servants Of God

We became pregnant shortly after being married and I had his first and my second child in 1993. We both were saved and gave our hearts to the Lord at the same ministry. Mine confession was 1989 and Chris was 1990. Mega-Mega Ministries was our church and we sat under the leadership of our pastor, Apostle Roland Roman.

I remember the day he sat us down to share his desire to see us work in ministry. Apostle began by reading scripture concerning ministry and the work of it. Interestingly, my husband was a jack of many trades, mechanics, electrical work and being a handy man. He could do a lot and pastor thought we would best serve together in the transportation ministry. Our role was to provide transportation to those who lived in Far Rockaway, NY that attended the church.

We learned that in ministry one must always be prepared when the phone rang. My husband Chris was often called at the last minute. Even if we had plans and pastor called, we would cancel them to tend to the needs of the ministry. It was a full-time job. That was our sacrifice to God and I supported it. I understood that my husband became a trustworthy servant, one who God and Apostle could count on, at first. When Chris received calls, my thoughts were, 'okay, this is what he has to do. No problem.' However, at the time, I didn't know my view would change.

The Mask of Resentment

Like a true father, Pastor Roman did everything in his power to lead and guide us in a lifestyle pleasing to the Lord.

By God's design, I was handpicked by an Elder for a particular work in Mega-Mega. She said to me, "The Lord has been dealing with me concerning you and being a servant on the prayer line." Hearing this wasn't easy to digest but I submitted and agreed to participate. I worked (volunteered) on the prayer line from noon to 6:00 p.m. Monday through Friday. Meanwhile, I had to balance being a wife, stay at home mother, and working in the ministry. Very often, I suffered loneliness and felt abandoned raising our children.

Literally, I hid behind the mask my make-up provided for me. As a woman in ministry, I was always put together, dressed properly and was known to keep my face, beat as they say, intact. Simply put, I was flawless. Outwardly, it appeared that life was good having a husband that was saved and a servant. However, I really didn't like our life sometimes. I hid deep down inside that I was aching and miserable. I felt like the church invaded my life to the point where I couldn't do other things. I wanted more time with my husband. I wanted to enjoy our children together. I wanted more family time, to travel, to sit around and do nothing sometimes. You know the simple things that other people do. Resentment slowly crept in.

There was no balance. I attended church three to four times a week. Once a year, we had a two-week vacation. Unbeknownst to me at that time, I was walking with a spirit of religion.

Nevertheless, I believed he was authentic and committed in his walk with Christ. Because we both said yes to God, I trusted and followed his lead for our family.

One night I asked my husband, "honey, what is my purpose?" He replied, "Your purpose is to help and serve me in my calling." I was satisfied with his reply. This was my biggest mistake, but I didn't realize it at that time, so I followed his instruction.

Lesson Learned: *Real Beauty is not what the eyes can behold, but what the heart can hold. What we see with our eyes will vanish someday. But what we store in our hearts will forever stay.*

THE AWAKENING

> Awake, O sleeper, and rise up from the dead; and Christ shall give you light." (Ephesians 5:14 TLB)

I continued to serve on the prayer line and I believed that I was called to do just and only that. That's it! Nothing more, nothing less, but I wasn't prepared of what would happen during one of my days of service. One Tuesday morning at the churches' Faith Clinic, a minister called me out and asked me, "Why aren't you preaching?" I replied, me? She answered, "Yes!" I replied, "No, I don't want to preach." She resumed telling me that my *yes* is connected to my family's salvation. Today you're going to give God a *yes*. That's when

I realized I was called to do something more within ministry. I yielded to what the Elder said but I didn't quite understand because I figured Chris had ministry covered enough for the both of us.

Eyes Wide Shut

When serving in ministry with Chris, the furthest thing from my mind is that he would do something to hurt me or our family. Why would he? He loves God! He loves me! He loves his children! Of course, he would never do anything to jeopardize what we have, right?

Mega-Mega Ministries was known for their tent revivals in the summer. People came from far and wide to attend. This was a high time in the Lord where those in attendance were healed, delivered and set free. The Holy Spirit was always heavy, present and revealed the good, bad, and ugly (casting out of demons) in some.

One night at the tent, there was this powerful woman preacher. Sadly, I don't remember her name, nor do I remember her message title, but I do remember one particular thing she said and the series of events that would occur after.

The woman of God said, "Leave these men in ministry alone!" She proceeded to call out specific men's names. She also called the men and elders of the church, including, Elder Roman (Apostle Son) and my husband Chris. Basically, the Holy Spirit revealed to her that women in the church were being inappropriate, flirtatious, or whatever you could think of to men within our church that were married.

Wow! Immediately, my eyes opened. I began thinking about all the women who were constantly around my husband and depending on him for certain things. Whenever I called he picked up the phone so I never questioned anything.

When Chris called me, I picked up as well. He would say things like, "I'm here taking sister so and so to here or honey, I'm coming home late."

The Mask of Naiveté

From that sermon, I realized due to all his responsibilities, I was masked in being naïve. God showed me that Chris wasn't who I thought he was. I couldn't prove it but I knew from that moment he had been unfaithful to me and our family and that's why God called him out.

After that night I became watchful of his actions, and I realized that he was coming home late. I noticed the repetitiveness of him coming home at 4:00 a.m., so I would ask him "Why are you coming home so late?" He made up a world of excuses. I never followed him or tried to investigate, I simply didn't have the energy for that. However, I went on for a little while being the naïve loving wife.

A popular and powerful woman of God was visiting our church. The event was over, it was time for us to go home and a member walks to Chris and says she needs him to drive her home. I said, "Why does she need you to drive her home? She can go home on the local van." I don't know what came over me but I knew something wasn't right between them. I would soon learn that you can hide all you want, but you can't hide from God. He is a protector of His children. Though some discoveries may hurt you to the core, the Lord will orchestrate moments that are only revealed to help you.

Exposed

It was Watch Night (New Year's Eve Service) and a young girl came running toward the building with a knife, and said, "You raped me, and you slept with my mother." To remove the commotion from in front of the church, Chris ran down the block, the girl followed and no one could hear what happened after. However, one person, a trusted source, heard enough to call and tell me. Chris knew that Apostle Roman would find out so he came home later that night and confessed to me.

He admitted to having sex with a woman at the church. He claimed it only happened once. This was very hard for me to take in. How could he do this to me? On bended knees, he cried and pleaded for my forgiveness. He told me the full truth. Not only was he having an affair with a woman from the church, but he also was having an affair with her daughter at the same time. This had been going on for four years. That meant my husband was not only an infidel, but a pedophile. Her daughter was only 14 years of age. At this point we had been married for well over ten years, had built a life with our children, and purchased a home.

I sat in the chair while he confessed to me. It felt like someone stabbed me in the stomach with a katana blade. I cried so hard that I couldn't see anything. It was all a blur. The pain was so excruciating and blood rushed to my head. I was filled with anger and rage. I wanted to kill him! He broke our vows and my heart was ripped into pieces. I was devastated, hurt, and traumatized. I asked myself many times, "Why would God allow this to happen to me?" What did I do wrong to deserve this? Continuously day and night I was traumatized by his words and betrayal.

The Best Kept Secret

The ability to keep a secret can be a good attribute for an individual to have. Let's be honest, no one wants their business to be spread by someone they trusted to be vulnerable with. However, certain secrets are bad and unless you are a priest telling judge, there should be a push to tell or encourage the person who is the offender in the secret to come clean. Confession cleanses the soul.

Keeping dirty secrets is a virus that spreads sickness. The offender person keeping the secret has to keep lying to maintain the integrity of the wrongdoing. Those around who know about the secret can experience anxiety, stress, depression, and much more. Dirty secrets destroy trust and relationships.

Sadly, in my case, the most revolting truth of all was that the leadership (the pastors, elders, and other in positions) which I served with for over ten years knew what Chris was doing. NO ONE told me! I never confronted those who knew about this woman and her daughter; the church took care of that. They had a meeting with her and she disappeared.

The only person I don't believe knew was Apostle Roman. However, once I realized who did, and some of who I considered to be good friends, did, from that point I wanted nothing to do with Chris, the church and God. Therefore, I left Chris and decided never to return to the house of God.

A mentor and confidant found out what happened and offered for me to stay with her. She said during that time, I needed my space to think, pray and not hear any comments or suggestions from anyone about what I should do. She told Chris that

I would be at her house and that he should make arrangements for someone to take care of the children. I went to stay for a few weeks.

During my time away, very few people from church contacted me to see if I was okay. The failure to reach out to me further confirmed why I didn't want to go back there. In hindsight, what can you say to someone whom you don't understand their pain? I don't think that many could've ministered to me in my devastated state. However, Abigail Roman, Elders Roman's wife, would call me every evening between 5:00 and 5:30 p.m. and sing to me.

A Heavy Mask

Eventually I went home and was encouraged to go back to church and hold my head up high.

The mask for that was too heavy on my face because my brain was filled with torment. I couldn't help but dwell on what happened, wonder what were people thinking and re-live the pain of knowing that I was the product of a 'best kept secret.'

Chris had an attitude of remorse but not for long. When we attended church together I could still see the residue of him messing around with other women. It was like I saw visions of him. There was no trust and I questioned him a lot about where he was going and who was he with.

There was no real change. He began staying out late again. I spoke to pastor and there were no consequences. Chris continued to serve in church. It's as if everyone was saying, "Okay, that happened but sis get over it!" My thoughts were, 'if this is what ministry is about, I don't want any parts of it. I was done!

INSTINCT

Job 38:26 (TLB) records, "*Who gives intuition and instinct?*" A woman's instinct is never wrong. The teenager was always around my husband. I knew that something was not right. And I asked my husband about her. Every time she would come around me, I would constantly hear his words "She is like a daughter to me".

These words were my real-life nightmare that triggered my behavior. Depressed and with feelings of rejection, my coping mechanism became alcohol, cocaine, and sex. This lifestyle took the pain away, or should I say, I thought it did, but in reality, it did not. Once I became sober, the pain emerged again and the torment continued.

I thank God he kept my mind from becoming mentally deranged, unable to think clearly or behave incontrollable which could have led to mental illness. God kept a hedge of protection around me and set a watch over my mind from suicidal thoughts which tormented me daily. As a result, I became a functional alcoholic for ten straight years.

The Destructive Mask

When going through mental turmoil of depression, torment, and outlandish thoughts, to escape one may participate in destructive behavior. I was a functioning bag of hurt that went to work daily at a NY State hospital, and looked for love and acceptance in all the wrong places at night. Moscato, Tequila and Vodka were my drinks of choice. My lunch breaks were filled with cocaine and cigarette parties in my car. On the weekends, I really let loose hitting the club surfing for Mr. Wrong. I never had a problem with men pursuing me; however strangely, I preferred to be the aggressor. I got what I wanted from them and threw them away when done. I had no remorse and didn't care. I believe I could function better if I felt numb and empty.

The next phase of destruction went from me being the pursuer to any man who told me I was pretty or beautiful, I fell for. I was still married, living in the main part of our house with the children and Chris was living downstairs. Basically, we lived together but were apart. I later found out that he stopped paying the mortgage and our house was in foreclosure.

While on my destructive seek, I found what I thought I was looking for in a man named Carson at my job. We began messing around heavy and having sex. The result, I got pregnant. At this point, Chris had left our home. When he discovered I was with child that was the ammunition he needed. He spread throughout the church that I was an adulterer and got pregnant by another man while still married to him.

Moving Forward

Though my heart wasn't there, I still attended church from time to time. One day while there, one of the mothers pulled me to the side and said, "Go back to your husband. Who's going to help you raise those boys? I know you are pregnant. You both did wrong. Start a new life." I listened to what she said and called Chris saying, "Let's start over new. I did wrong. You did wrong." He replied, "Okay, yeah, no problem. I'll be back on Monday."

Chris never came on Monday. I called to the point of blowing up his phone and he didn't answer. While holding the phone, my oldest son comes to me and says, "Mom, dad isn't coming back. He is with Sister Linda." Dang, another katana blade in my stomach! My son went on to say, "Dad has been living with her." In shock, I called Apostle Roman and said, "Are you aware that my husband is living with Sister Linda? I'm trying to make my marriage work. I understand what I did was wrong, being pregnant by another man. We had a conversation and all of a sudden he isn't picking up the phone like he doesn't want to be bothered with me. Now I find out that he is living with a woman who sings on the praise and worship team at church?" Pastor responded, "Chris told me that he was working with her on an album." I replied, "IT'S A LIE!" Pastor ensured he would speak to Chris and straighten everything out, but nothing happened. He lived with that woman for eight years.

I had my baby boy in 2004 and began proceedings to divorce. I developed a closer relationship with my child's father and we moved in together. The scandal continued with Chris, in 2005 he had a child on Linda with a very young girl at the church. Finally, the church leadership realized there was a problem. Despite the baby, Linda stayed with him and everybody thought Chris was going to marry her. Once our divorce was final, he remarried a woman he claimed that God told him to marry during a 5:00 a.m. prayer meeting.

As you can imagine during this whole ordeal, our children were confused and torn between us as parents. Sadly Chris never came back to me, and I would eventually deal with the consequences of our break up. However, I never thought he wouldn't come around for his children. All communication stopped. I tried to mend them but Chris wasn't interested. Eventually, I let the matter go. His lack of action hurt them deeply and would yield not so good results to come.

CHAPTER TWO

UNNECESSARY STORMS

> For I know that nothing good lives in me, that is, in my flesh [my human nature, my worldliness—my sinful capacity]. For the willingness [to do good] is present in me, but the doing of the good is not. (Romans 7:18 AMP)

Living in a dark and lonely place, I became angry at the church and angry at God. My ex-husband refused to co-parent and pay child support. My outlook and perspective on life were negative and hostile. I trusted no one but bills needed to be paid and I had to survive. Therefore, I yielded to my flesh. I loved and obeyed it. I developed a closer relationship with Carson, the man I became pregnant by while married to Chris. My home was saved from foreclosure and he moved in with us to be closer to his son but also to help me raise my boys.

The Mask of Happiness

We lived together unmarried for five years. I knew it wasn't God's will. Nevertheless, I settled for this illusion of happiness and continued to embrace my unresolved inner torment. Ignoring the truth of this lifestyle was shoved to the far reaches of my mind.

As time passed, I found myself stuck and I couldn't find my way out. My disobedience caused yet another layer of inner turmoil. In my heart, I asked the Lord "How do I get out of this relationship?" Living in sin never has a good ending. I was reminded of the scripture that Apostle Roman shared in Hebrews 11:25, which states, "Choosing rather to suffer affliction with the people of God, then to enjoy the pleasures of sin for a season."

We worked at the same job but he was terminated. I never got the full story, however, he became a stay at home parent. He got our son off to school, cooked all the meals, washed clothes, cleaned the house, and was there when needed. I didn't have to worry about anything. My role was to go to work and make sure the bills were paid. Though we were living in sin, unmarried, everything was fine! Right?

I had a tenant who lived on the first floor of my house. Martha, who was Hispanic, and had a boy and a girl. She was beautiful and seemed like a really nice lady. She was a good tenant who paid her rent on time. I never suspected anything; however I did work at night and often did double shifts.

One day Martha comes to me and shares that Carson had been coming downstairs to rape her. Now that was a strong word and I didn't buy it for one second. I immediately corrected her and said, "It's not rape! Y'all are having sex in your apartment. However, I am glad you brought this to my attention." I didn't get irate; I simply made the decision to put him out. My thoughts were, 'why put her out when her rent pays the mortgage.' My mask of happiness was shattered to pieces but my way of escape was front and center.

Cheating Carson

I immediately confronted my son's father and the conversation went as follows.

"Carson, Martha said that you've been raping her."

He replies, "Why would I want to?"

I said, "Yeah, why would you when y'all are actually having sex?"

Without looking me straight in the eye, He replied, "Oh, she's a liar."

> Isn't it funny how you recall things you didn't pay attention to previously?

I went on to say, "Oh my God, you got that girl pregnant. I remember her telling me she had an abortion. Now why would she tell me that? I'm her landlord, not her friend, so her personal life is none of my business."

Carson continued to deny it but I knew he was lying. I told him that he had to leave.

That night, after the children went to bed, Carson came into our room with a gun in his hand saying, "If I can't live or stay with you, I'm going to take my life." The look in his eyes was almost demonic and I realized that he was serious. I had to think quickly on how to talk him down before he killed us both. My training from working in a psychiatric hospital had to kick in. For a moment, I couldn't see him as my son's father; I had to see him as a patient. In a calm voice,

"Carson, why would you want to kill yourself?"

"Because Shirley, you are trying to leave me. I can't have that."

"Carson, you don't want to kill yourself in front of my kids or your son."

"YES I DO AND I WILL!"

"Okay, let's calm down and talk about this. Look, I was upset about what Martha told me and I overreacted. We can get through this and I no longer want you to leave. Let's work it out and continue to raise our son together. Can you give me the gun so I can put it away? Come on Carson, it will be okay. I will make Martha leave in the morning, okay?"

He gave me the gun and went to bed. While he was asleep, I called his father and mother telling them Carson had to leave that night. His brother, (a corrections officer) and his wife came to get him. I woke him from sleeping. He saw his brother and asked, "What is he doing here?" I answered, "He is here to take you home. I should call the police but I won't because your brother has asked me not to. Just leave and we can move on like this never happened." He left that night to go and live with his parents.

I was numb. I felt no emotion because my heart was hardened. At that moment, I vowed to never love again. However, I also realized my anger and unforgiveness towards my ex-husband caused an unnecessary storm. I realized that the most dangerous pain is the one you cannot feel.

SECOND TIME AROUND

Save me, O God! For the waters have come up to my neck. I sink in deep mire,

Where there is no standing; I have come into deep waters, Where the floods overflow me. I am weary with my crying; My throat is dry; My eyes fail while I wait for my God. (Psalm 69:1, 2)

Two years later, I met Warren. I was good friends with his sister Wanda. Her children went to school with mine. We were like family and lived in the same neighborhood.

It was during the Christmas holiday, I was visiting her house with my children and her brother was there. Wanda introduced us, but shortly after I left. I had no idea he was interested in me and I wasn't thinking about him. However, about 30 minutes later Warren came to knock on my door. He stated that he didn't want to speak to me in front of his family so he asked his sister where I lived. I was flattered by what he did and we engaged in conversation.

Wily Warren

Warren was tall, dark skin, very built where his size commanded attention. He was retired from the Army and resided in Georgia. He quickly broke down that wall I put up from Carson. He was a true gentleman. I never had anyone treat me the way he did, not even my ex-husband. Opening doors, cards, candy, flowers, clothes, traveling, and fine restaurants was what he provided. First class, royal treatment and I felt like a queen around him. I would go to Georgia to visit and he would come to New York to see me. We went on to date for six months.

Valentine's Day was approaching and he asked, "Are you coming for Valentine's Day?" I answered, "I'm not sure if I can get the time off from work." He replied, "Well, I really need you to get that time off." I asked, "Why?" He answered, "Because I want us to get married." I almost dropped the telephone and fainted. That moment was overwhelming. He went on to say, "You don't have to give me an answer now but I want us to get married." Warren began to flood my ears with how he fell in love with me and believed that we could make our relationship work. He had it all planned out. Good God all day! What woman doesn't love a man with a plan?

"Come and stay in Georgia. You can always go back and visit your family. Leave the house to your sons." My thoughts were, 'is this too good to be true? Did I finally meet the right man for me? This is a blessing. I can go to Georgia, relax and continue to be treated like a queen. This, absolutely, has to be God." I was in my mind and not the mind of Christ. Two days later I called Warren back and said, "Yes, I will marry you."

The Controlling Mask

His formal/informal proposal was in February and we married in a small chapel, in March. It was just he and I and his best friend. My boys didn't want to come and no one in my family could attend on such a short notice. As long as I was happy, they were good. Although I still dabbled with drugs and alcohol, this was a chance for a new start. Warren wasn't aware of the addictions. I was able to keep it all under control.

The plan was I would first take a leave of absence first, quit my job by September and fully move to live with my husband. However, in April, May and June, I got to know him better and decided that I wanted a divorce.

Sadly, the person who I dated wasn't the person I married. They say when you meet someone, they send their representative. Well, that's exactly what happened to me. Once I said I do, everything changed.

Warren was possessive, constantly angry, verbally abusive, and I couldn't make a move without him breathing down my neck. It was like I was in prison. I also realized, from my training of working in a psychiatric hospital, he displayed signs of being Bipolar and possibly undiagnosed mentally ill. My husband never hit me but I was definitely in a domestic violence situation.

"Lord Jesus, once and again, please get me out of this!" A plan and my help came swiftly.

I told Warren that I had to travel back to New York to tie of some business concerning my house. My plan was to file for divorce then since his temperament was always off. While there, my friend (Fontaine) husband Fred noticed a conversation between Warren and another man on Facebook. The conversation went as follows,

"Hey Warren, how is Dennis?"

Warren replied, "Dennis and I are good. We are working it out and getting back together."

Fred goes to Fontaine and alerts her of the conversation and says,

"Isn't this Shirley's husband?"

Fontaine replies, "Oh my goodness, yes!"

Fred and Fontaine called me over to their house. When they opened the door, a look of trouble appeared on their faces. My thoughts were, "Who died?" They asked me to have a seat because they had something to tell me. Fred proceeded to share screenshots of the conversation between Warren and the other person. Fred goes on to say,

"Do you know about this person? Have you ever met Warren's friend," showing me his picture.

I replied, "I don't know him and never met him."

He replied, "Are you sure?"

I said, "Yes!"

Fred told me to read the conversation closer and I couldn't believe my eyes. Oh my God, I'm married to a man whose in a relationship with another man.

This Can't Be My Life

I called Warren on the telephone to confront him about the gentleman and the conversation. He claimed he didn't know what I was talking about. He hung up. However, he immediately blocked me from seeing his account on Facebook. Not only did he block me, he blocked all of our mutual friends and my family.

I began texting him and said, "Oh my God, I never knew you were living this life. I never knew you were gay or bi-sexual." He never confirmed or denied. We never talked about it again. It was as if nothing happened in his eyes but I was done.

I filed for divorce in New York and had him served in Georgia. Once received, he cussed me out with perfection. I wasn't offended at all. I told him, "Please just sign the papers and we can both go on with our lives. We've been married for only three months, we don't have any property or children together, just sign it!" Warren tried to get me back to Georgia to file but I consulted with a judge who told me I wasn't required. I didn't budge and eventually our contested divorce became final.

The Familiar Mask

Heartbroken and devastated, I quickly put on the mask I knew best. My addictive behaviors spun out of control. Heavy drinking, destructive behavior, and everything in between were home for me. Sadly, my youngest son had to witness it all. When was this vicious cycle going to end?

FIGHTING IN THE FLESH - A LOSING BATTLE

> For we do not wrestle against flesh and blood, but against principalities, against powers, against the rulers of the darkness of this age, against spiritual hosts of wickedness in the heavenly places. (Ephesians 6:12 NKJV)

Have you ever felt like religion overtook your relationship with God? I have. My memories of serving were frustrating and depressing. It was like a recorder that the enemy played nonstop in my mind the horrible things I experienced. This caused me to lose focus and bask in my hurt and pain. I felt I had nowhere to turn. Nevertheless, I did have two choices. I could turn from my wicked ways and serve God or continue in my life of sin.

I sensed the hand of God drawing me back to Him, but yet I refused to answer the call. I struggled with walking in my God-given purpose because I was preoccupied with embracing my pain.

I remained in a stuck place hiding behind the various masks of make-up and suffered in silence.

During my distress, God continued to reach out to me. I would hear Him say, "I HAVE NEED OF THEE, I LOVE YOU, SURRENDER TO ME." There were nights I would cry my eyes out, yet I still rejected God.

Even though I was out of the will of God, He continued to provide for me and my children. He kept me in my home for 21 years without paying a mortgage! He had a purpose for me despite my disobedience and willingness to submit. God never stopped loving me unconditionally. He has proven his love and he remained faithful. I was living in his F.O.G. (the favor of God).

THE VISITATION

Behold, I stand at the door and knock. If anyone hears My voice and opens the door, I will come into him and dine with him, and he with Me. (Revelation 3:20)

I was working the graveyard shift around 4:00.a.m, at Pilgrim Psychiatric Hospital and had a dream/vision. Pastor Roman and an Elder pulled up a chair and sat next to me. My pastor said, "*it's time to come back.*" And I replied with tears in my eyes, "*No I don't want to come back.*" He repeated it again and I replied the same way. He looked me in my eyes and said "*Daughter, I never did those things to you. I never betrayed you nor did I ever hurt you, I'm not like man. I never left you! Nothing can separate my love from you. I have a plan for you and great things in store for you. But if you choose not to come back, this year your sons will bury you.*"

At that point, I woke up and started to weep. I knew I had to make a decision to live for God or die prematurely and abort my calling and purpose on earth. I hastened to repentance with tears in my eyes. I humbled myself and asked God, "*Take me back to my first love*".

For the first time after 10 years of hurt, pain, rejection, abandonment, and anger, I realized that God was there all along and I felt embraced by His love. This was my new beginning.

CHAPTER THREE

BLAMELESS

> Whoever believes and has decided to trust in Him [as personal Savior and Lord] is not judged [for this one, there is no judgment, no rejection, no condemnation. (John 3:18 AMP)

After all I had been through, I finally made the decision to serve God. Before I could serve Him, I had to admit a few things I didn't want to come to terms with in the past.

1. I had a problem with alcohol addiction.
2. I had a problem with fornication.
3. I had to stop hiding and tell God, directly, my problem.

The Bible says in 1 John 1:9, "If we confess our sins, He is faithful and just to forgive us our sins and to cleanse us from all unrighteousness." This means that only God can deliver us from any and all unrighteousness if we seek and ask. I often heard that "God is a keeper," but hearing it isn't enough. I had to experience His keeping power to sustain because my flesh was constantly in a place of fire that had a revolving door. I would do something, ask God to forgive me and go back to do the same thing. I kept boxes and cases of Moscato bottles in my house.

So I confessed, repented and the urge for drugs and to fornicate, ceased immediately. Seeking God, His word, and to be a better person increased. My youngest son noticed the drastic change in me and said, "You really are taking this serious. I haven't seen you take a drink in a while." I didn't realize he was watching me.

Some Masks Are Good

Some people describe having certain encounters with God that led them to stop a habit or addiction. However, that wasn't the case from me. No angel descended. God didn't speak to me in an audible voice. **I simply made a decision!** I didn't want to live my life that way anymore and the Lord met me when I shifted my focus to Him, fasting and praying.

One day I was led to call an old and dear friend named Jonathan. I felt the tug that God was leading me to form some type of ministry and I needed an ear and to talk to someone I trusted. In the middle of our conversation, he said,

"You know that you are called to women, correct?"

I replied, "Yes."

He went on to say, "God is saying that you are to minister to women."

I replied, "Yes, because she (the woman) is me."

He became quiet for a moment and said, "We need to consecrate for this one."

The Mask of Healing and Ministry

From that conversation I believed that I would reach a lot of women who were silently suffering in ministry and life, but could not freely articulate what they were feeling. At the point of our conversation, ten years had passed of hurt, headaches, heartaches, and then the walk toward total healing.

From that consecration and conversation, in 2018 God led me to birth a women's ministry called S.H.E. - Serving Herself with Excellence. This ministry is about encouraging and empowering women who endured pain behind their make-up moments. It is also a ministry of reformation and reconciliation. Allow me a moment to explain what that means.

The ministry of reconciliation is for the person who was once with God but left. When they return, God shows His love and receive them back despite what you've said, done or walked through. This is one of the many reasons why Jesus died on the cross, to reconcile man back to God. The ministry of reformation is for the person who needs to transform, meaning, this will take place in your mind, heart and actions. Transformation + Renewal = Reformation.

My conversations with Jonathan continued, he agreed to be the administrator of the ministry. It's a blessing to converse with someone who can pull the gifts you have out. I understood that I was part of the body of Christ but didn't fit in the church building nor did I feel that I spoke eloquent enough for such a big task. However, Jonathan further spoke into my life and said, "You are going back to school. If you don't feel comfortable, you can take speech classes. Don't worry about that. You are called to the people who are lost in the streets. God has a set people who are ready to hear what you have to say because you come from where they are. You will reach them on their level." I took what my good friend said, believed God and ran with it. The Lord gave me a heart for evangelism and lost souls.

A Student of the Word

The Lord took me on a journey to dig much deeper into His Word. The 'Excellence' part of the ministry had to prevail, in that I needed to know the word. This led to me begin studying the women in the Bible. I studied Mary and Elizabeth, Abigail, and Gomer. This led me to create an event for women.

During the process of cultivating my ministry, I facilitated two awesome events before the 2020 pandemic. To God Be the Glory! At this time, I also was grieving the loss of my aunt and mother who passed within three months apart that year.

Amid my mother transitioning, I was grief-stricken yet I had to move forward and stay focused.

Due to the loss of my mother, I felt emotionally empty and extremely lonely with no one to talk to. My house was being renovated and I opened up to my contractor who was working on my property. Needless to say, it led to a road of destruction.

CHICANERY

Even my own familiar friend in whom I trusted,
Who ate my bread,
Has lifted up his heel against me. (Psalm 41:9)

Webster defines chicanery as "one who uses trickery or dishonest means to deceive or achieve some purpose."

False Frankie

One day I was in a beauty supply store trying on and looking to purchase a wig for an event. As I proceeded to look in the mirror, a gentleman came by where I was standing and said,

"That's the one. It looks very nice on you."

A little shocked, I asked, "How would a man know?"

He replied, "I previously owned several beauty shops, so I am used to women and hair."

Okay, he got my attention.

He then pulled out his card and said, "Not only did I own a beauty shop, I am a licensed contractor." The card had a picture of before and after redoing a kitchen.

I said, "Wow, I do need a contractor, for my rental property needs repairs."

He replied, "I can come by and give you an estimate."

I agreed.

Frankie came to my house to give an estimate but it turned into a conversation on where I could save money within the house. Then, he made his move to ask me out on a date to the movies. I agreed.

First, he finessed his way by calling and having conversations with me. Personality wise, I thought he was a nice guy. Phone conversations turned in to check in visits, those turned into going out to dinner, all of it turned into seeing him every day.

We got to know each other and he stated he was divorced. His presence helped me to overcome depression from the loss of my mother. I was able to breathe. I felt alive once again. He cooked for me. He made me laugh. He was the one who whispered in my ear, "You're loved. You're beautiful. You're needed!" Yes, I sunk right into the quicksand. We went out every day, but I felt in my heart something wasn't right. It was too good to be true but I was already emotionally attached to him.

There were times we were out and I would hear the Lord whispering in my ear, *the blessings of the Lord makes rich and adds no sorrow.* Other times I heard the words of Apostle Roman saying, "You don't marry the house, you marry what's in the house!"

The Lying Mask

One day, we had a conversation about family, life, etc. I asked Frankie,

"What year did you get your divorce?" The room went silent. So I asked again.

He replied, "I never told you I was divorced. I told you I was separated for seven years."

Once again I was deceived. He presented himself as a single man. I saw him on every major holiday and we spent his birthday together. When you can't see a man during those times, it's a telltale sign that someone else is in the picture. However, everything in my gut of uneasiness was revealed upon his confession. I had further questions like,

1. Why his phone never rung when he was with me?
2. Why he would stay late at my house but never pushed the issue to spend the night?

My God! How did I open the door to repeat this cycle? Just for a moment, I really felt that I was in a relationship with someone I could trust. The truth presented itself. I'm forever grateful for God's grace and mercy! I had to make a decision. I left him but he didn't leave me. It wasn't that easy. I had a soul-tie with a man I thought I had a future with. I struggled with his words, "I will leave her just give me some time. He even presented me with separation papers to convince me that he had no ties with his wife.

While in prayer one morning crying in repentance before God, I asked him to give me his strength to overcome! I had to realize my worth. I came too far to have another setback. God dealt with me and said, "Now you know. So, Shirley, are you going to stay in a relationship that I would never come into agreement with or will you let it go?" I knew that God wouldn't override my will so I had to make a decision.

Side Bar

If you are ever in a position where you have to make a decision about leaving someone in an ungodly relationship where one is married, here are a few questions to ask yourself.

1. Do I love God enough to obey him?
2. Do I love God enough to let the relationship go?
3. Do I value myself as a woman?
4. Was I taught better than this?

The truth is there was no guarantee I would survive another deceptive tactic and needed to end our ungodly relationship. Frankie tried to seduce me in many ways to get me to change my mind. He tried to convince me to settle and compromise my morals. As much as I wanted him, I couldn't lower my standards because I knew the truth and had to defend it. I had to love myself enough to see that I was worth more than being number two. Being second does not look good on me! I know when God sends me someone he's not going to send me second best. Besides, after seven years he couldn't get a divorce? That made no sense to me. I understood that being the other woman doesn't make me #1, it makes me lose. You lose your self-esteem, your values, and your character. You do not receive love. You inherit lies, deceit, and stolen affections that didn't belong to you.

CAUTION: Single women please stop trying to give therapy to a married man. It's one thing to be wanted but another thing to be valued. Being wanted is a human emotion that can be skewed into something that looks like, sounds like, and walks like that special person to fulfill that special place in your heart. However, it is not what you bargained for because being valued is love.

CHAPTER FOUR

FORGIVENESS / FORGIVING YOURSELF / FORGIVING OTHERS

> ...bearing with one another, and forgiving one another, if anyone has a complaint against another; even as Christ forgave you, so you also must do. (Colossians 3:13)

Many have a hard time believing in God's forgiveness. We may think that after all we've done how anyone can completely forgive. What are your thoughts about this personally? Maybe you feel that you have done some horrible things. Even if you could be forgiven, who can ever forget the things you've done? Part of the recovery process is accepting complete forgiveness from God.

We may keep track of our failures, but God does not keep lists of our past sins. In his eyes we are clean. I challenge you to step out of your comfort zone and allow God to turn your scars into stars! During my journey, I was faced with the decision to forgive or not forgive the situation with my ex-husband Charismatic Chris.

One day Chris reached out to me sharing that he fell on hard times and needed a place to stay. He asked if he could stay in my rental property for six months while he got back on his feet. There we were! The person who jeopardized me and my children's shelter when he stopped paying the mortgage now needed a place to stay.

The Forgiveness Test

There are steps to forgiveness. When hurt, but have professed you want to be a different person in God, he will put you to the test. Contrary to how many leaders of faith teach this topic, to forgive is a process and one that doesn't happen overnight. What are the steps?

- ✓ Acknowledge
- ✓ Think
- ✓ Accept
- ✓ Determine

✓ Repair
✓ Learn
✓ Forgive

Acknowledge everything that happened during the offense. Write it down or speak to someone if you need to. **Think** about what happened and what didn't. It's not about rehearsing what happened or what you could've done differently to prevent the offense; it's about getting you to the next step. **Accept** what happened and the fact that you cannot change what occurred. It's the past. **Determine** what you are going to do now. Will you or won't you forgive the person? At this point, it's a matter of choice. **Repair** your heart and mind. This can be done by scripture, praying, speaking to a therapist, the goal is to heal. **Learn** from the situation. Everything we go through has a learning component. We must be willing to learn from all experiences good and bad. **Forgive!** First, forgive yourself for what happened. Oftentimes we don't forgive ourselves because we question why we allowed the offense to take place. Then, we are angry and hurt because of what happened. Let's go to the word which shows us how to forgive.

"Look on my affliction and my pain, And forgive all my sins." – Psalm 25:18

"Have mercy on me, O God, according to Your lovingkindness;

According to the greatness of Your compassion blot out my transgressions.

² Wash me thoroughly from my wickedness and guilt

And cleanse me from my sin.

³ For I am conscious of my transgressions and I acknowledge them;

My sin is always before me.

⁴ Against You, You only, have I sinned

And done that which is evil in Your sight,

So that You are justified when You speak [Your sentence]

And faultless in Your judgment.

⁵ I was brought forth in [a state of] wickedness;

In sin my mother conceived me [and from my beginning I, too, was sinful].

⁶ Behold, You desire truth in the innermost being,

And in the hidden part [of my heart] You will make me know wisdom.

7 Purify me with [a]hyssop, and I will be clean;
Wash me, and I will be whiter than snow.
8 Make me hear joy and gladness and be satisfied;
Let the bones which You have broken rejoice.
9 Hide Your face from my sins
And blot out all my iniquities.
10 Create in me a clean heart, O God,
And renew a right and steadfast spirit within me.
11 Do not cast me away from Your presence
And do not take Your Holy Spirit from me." –
Psalm 51:1-11AMP

"If we confess our sins, He is faithful and just to **forgive** us our sins and to cleanse us from all unrighteousness." – 1 John 1:9

"For if you **forgive** men their trespasses, your heavenly Father will also **forgive** you. But if you do not **forgive** men their trespasses, neither will your Father **forgive** your trespasses." – Matthew 6:14-15

Then Peter came to Him and said, "Lord, how often shall my brother sin against me, and I **forgive** him? Up to seven times?" – Matthew 18:21

Then Jesus said, "Father, **forgive** them, for they do not know what they do." And they divided His garments and cast lots. – Luke 23:34

Show and Prove

As I previously stated, Chris came to me asking for shelter. I said yes. With a forgiving heart, I allowed him to stay temporarily until he got on his feet and relocated.

Was I supposed to stay in the pit of hate and unforgiveness or rise up to the occasion to let it go and move on with my life? Honestly, it was not an easy process. I had made up my mind to become the best version that God desired for me. I refused to allow my past to keep me a prisoner. My past was just a lesson, not a death sentence. My past does not belong in my future.

Forgiveness can be one of the hardest things to do on your journey to achieve and remain in peace. Nonetheless, forgiving yourself can be the hardest of all. Psalm 32:5 states, *I acknowledged my sin to You, And my iniquity I have not hidden. I said, "I will confess my transgressions to the LORD," And You forgave the iniquity of my sin.*

After agreeing, Chris confessed that he couldn't live alone. In other words, he was struggling to be by himself. He further asked if his girlfriend could come and live with him. I told him, "You are a pastor and, no I will not allow you to live with your girlfriend in my home. You have to marry her" He married her. I charged him minimal rent and asked that he maintain the house with his fix it skills. Chris agreed and moved out at the six month agreement.

You may say to yourself some things are so damaging, they are beyond forgiveness. Forgiveness does not excuse what someone has done; it frees you from living life with the pain. Unforgiveness robs you of a life of freedom that God desires for you.

According to loveworthlivingfor.com, forgiveness requires our participation. W.M. Paul Young said in his book, *The Shack* that forgiveness is just releasing the person's neck from your hand.

Remember the other woman who cheated with my ex-husband? She called me asking for forgiveness. She repented from all her indiscretions. I humbly accepted. God restored our relationship as if it never happened!

In my walk with the Lord, I noticed two sets of words that leaders have a problem saying: I'm sorry and forgive me!

In our conversation with tears, the other woman stated that if I had not accepted her apology and had not forgiven her, she purposed in her heart to commit suicide. My brothers and sisters, it is so important to forgive ourselves and forgive one another. God never **asked** us to forgive. It's a requirement.

> "And whenever you stand praying, if you have anything against anyone, forgive him, that your Father in heaven may also forgive you your trespasses. (Mark 11:25).

Thus far you have read a lot about disobedience, betrayal, adultery, addiction and the many masks one can wear. However, Jesus is Love and the most important relationship in your life is a personal one with Jesus Christ. If you would like to receive Him as your Lord and Savior, (or rededicate) and enter into the greatest relationship you have ever known, please repeat this prayer with all sincerity in your heart.

Prayer of Salvation
Heavenly Father, you loved the world so much that you gave your only begotten Son to die for my sins and that whosoever believes in him will not perish but have eternal life. I believe in my heart and confess with my mouth that Jesus Christ is Lord. I believe you died on the cross for me and bore all my sins. I believe in my heart that you raised Jesus from the dead and that He is alive today. I am a sinner. I am sorry for my sins and I ask you to forgive me. By faith, I receive Jesus Christ now as my Lord and Savior. I believe through faith that I am saved and will spend eternity with you. Thank you Father. In Jesus name, Amen.

CHAPTER FIVE

THE PROCESS OF HEALING

He heals the brokenhearted And binds up their wounds [healing their pain and comforting their sorrow]. (Psalm 147:3 AMP)

The opening scripture of this chapter is Psalm 147. All Psalms in the Bible are special. They are love letters to God and can help us in our communication with the Lord as we go through our many issues and seasons of life. Psalm 147 teaches us how we should praise the Lord. In the beginning we are told to praise the Lord, then we are commanded to praise the Lord for His restorative mercies, we go on to learn how to praise the Lord for the joy He finds in His children. Finally, we are commanded to praise the Lord for His word.

In verse four, it says he heals us and binds up our wounds. I can attest that when you are hurt, broken down, feeling busted and completely disgusted, you cannot see how God can help or heal.

Dear reader, know that 'healing is a process' that takes time. First, I had to acknowledge that I needed healing to take place.

One day I was having a discussion with a friend about Alcoholics Anonymous, and she was explaining the 12 step point process. The principles are:

Honesty	Faith	Surrender
Soul Searching	Integrity	Acceptance
Humility	Willingness	Forgiveness
Maintenance	Making Contact	Service

I cannot fully detail or explain the process of how God took me through all of them, however, I can share important points I believe are significant and for the overall purpose of this book.

One day, I had a come to Jesus moment and a reality check. For many years, while walking with Jesus, I hid the pain and hurt, shame and rejection. I held on to unforgiveness and finally came to a moment of being tired of the inability to move forward in mind, body and spirit. I became exhausted that my relationship with God was continuously hindered because I held on to secrets that many possibly believed, were no longer an issue for me.

All Masks Off

So, I came into agreement with the Holy Spirit of God and the hidden parts were revealed. In other words, I was **honest** with God. I repented for all I was holding and asked God to turn my heart to flesh from stone. In other words, I chose **faith**, to **surrender** and to walk in **humility**. Over time, my heart was changed, my mind became one with Christ and I could see that without God, I could do nothing. I had to **accept** all that happened and understand that there wasn't much I could do to change it. They weren't all wrong, we all were.

Though he left and never came back, I had to forgive **Heart Crusher Corey**. He died some years later and the Lord had me to release him and understand that people will do things and you may never discover the reason why. In the case of **Charismatic Chris**, I had to stop blaming him for everything that happened. For a long time I acted like I forgave him, but every chance I got, I would blame shift and throw our previous situation up in his face. For **Cheating Carson**, our relationship was developed through adultery. I was still married! For, **Wily Warren**, I beat myself up at first about not seeing the signs. However, they were probably there all along. Was I blinded by all his gifts or was it I didn't want to see the signs? **False Frankie** was a repeated cycle. I once cheated on my husband Chris. Though in my mind our marriage was done, I shouldn't have entered in a relationship with another man without coming to a resolve in mine.

The truths are I had to **soul search** and take responsibility for my part. I had to take responsibility for the addictive behaviors I carried. I had to take responsibility for my healing.

To seal the deal, God led me back to the ministry where I experienced hurt, shame and rejection. You may ask why God would send me back to the house that caused me so much pain. For peace and sanity, forgiving everyone, including myself, was the key to move forward. As a result, God released me to another ministry where I was able to receive total and finite healing.

Willing to see myself, gradually, I gained my confidence in believing that with God all things are possible. My self-esteem started to rise and I started to believe in myself

God showed me that I kept repeating the same mistakes. I stop trying to figure everything out on my own and give it to God by *trusting in the Lord with all my heart and leaning not to my own understanding but acknowledging him in all my ways so He can direct my paths.* (Proverbs 3:5, 6) Letting go of my past and focusing on my true destiny was my aspiration. And . . . worship and praise became my lifestyle.

Healing is for you! Freedom is for you! It is better to be free from hurt and people than to be bound by it all.

I began to understand that my problematic journeys of ungodly relationships stemmed from insecurities, vulnerabilities, lack of self-love, and unforgiveness towards myself and others. These inadequacies were a cocktail for disaster and seeking God in the nuances of everyday life helped me to overcome the traps that at one time easily ensnared me. Self-care and healing became an integral part of my life to boost my confidence and identity as a whole woman.

Psalms 18:33 (AMP) tells us "He makes my feet like hinds' feet [able to stand firmly and tread safely on paths of testing and trouble]; He sets me [securely] upon my high places."

When you **surrender** your **will** and trust God, your bruises become your beauty marks. Every pain you ever experienced; every trial you ever walked through; every storm you ever endured, your end is sure without trusting and depending on God.

When the "YES LORD" came out of my spirit, life came forth. Love embraced me. Bitterness and anger turned into forgiveness and encouragement.

Isaiah 61:3 tells us *God gives us beauty for ashes, the oil of joy for mourning, the garment of praise for the spirit of heaviness.*

God often uses our deepest pain as the launching pad of our greatest calling!! Some women are lost in their fiery trials, but some women are built from it!! I became one of those women who were built from the fire!

BURN THE MASK

I believe that God has a purpose in all things and we should be a people of purpose. Everything I have walked through on my journey, I have learned that God meets us where we are and helps us get to where we need to be.

It would be a mistake for us to focus on a past chapter in our life. Chapter one is over. This is a new chapter and with each new chapter, is the opportunity for us to discover something fresh and new. Isaiah 43:18-19 states, *"Do not remember the former things, Nor consider the things of old. Behold, I will do a new thing, Now it shall spring forth; Shall you not know it? I will even make a way in the wilderness, And rivers in the desert"*

God loves us because He wants to, not because we deserve it. I've learned:

1. That being aware of God's love is the beginning of all healing and restoration.
2. To be more God-conscious instead of sin-conscious.
3. The importance of healing.
4. The unending love and grace of God. "The steadfast love of the Lord never ceases, God's mercies never come to an end" – Lamentation 3:22 RSV
5. Creating an environment of worship and praise helps His love to grow in me.
6. Meditating on His promises will help to boost my confidence and trust in Him.

One of my favorite scriptures is Jeremiah 29:11 which reads, *For I know the thoughts that I think toward you, says the LORD, thoughts of peace and not of evil, to give you an expected end.*

I am grateful for His steadfast love and faithfulness. After everything I have been through, He kept my mind from the mental institution and he covered ME! He revealed the many masks I was wearing or using and helped me to get rid myself of them all.

I understand all those things happened to me, but not for me! I can celebrate myself! What are my prayers for you?

1. You will trust the process of God!
2. To learn from my years of mistakes, struggles, and pain.
3. To learn that a life of disobedience is exhausting.
4. You will make a commitment to yourself to engage in self-care.
5. You will embrace your journey.
6. You will strive to understand who you are; why you do the things you do; and why you think the way you think.
7. You will keep exploring, learning, believing, giving, loving, and reaching to become all God created you to be.
8. If you have any masks, you will spiritually burn them all.

My past story is filled with abandonment, addiction, adultery, betrayal, disobedience, masks and lust. And perhaps your story is filled with some of the same.

When working with God to conquer our many issues, we can often feel like why or how can God use me? I've learned that God is sovereign and He can do what He wants, when He wants and with whom. For further study and reference, I point your attention to stories in the Bible where God mightily used those who others thought weren't good enough.

1. Jesus.
2. King David.
3. Moses.
4. Rahab.
5. The Apostle Paul (formerly known as Saul of Tarsus).
6. The woman at the well.

My unending prayer is that as you receive God's grace, favor, love, mercy, and forgiveness, you live boldly and become all that God intends for you. Live in the fullness of His joy and beauty he created in you.

ABOUT THE AUTHOR

Dr. Shirley Peoples, an apostolic voice established as a ministry gift for the gospel of Jesus Christ demonstrates with authority. Under her apostolic commission, she serves as an evangelist, teacher and prophet. Dr. Peoples serves as a catalyst in various facets of ministry as a counselor and mentor.

Her passion for people and especially women goes beyond the traditional walls of ministry. Her dedication is always demonstrated with love and compassion.

Dr. People's YES to God comes with a sincere commitment because she realizes that the transparency of her life experiences is a teaching tool for women in their quest to become whole.

For bookings and additional information:
www.drshirleypeoples.com.